BERLIN BURSTS

Also by Robert Sheppard

Poetry
Returns
Daylight Robbery
The Flashlight Sonata
Transit Depots/Empty Diaries
           (with John Seed [text] and Patricia Farrell [images])
Empty Diaries
The Lores
The Anti-Orpheus: a notebook
Tin Pan Arcadia
Hymns to the God in which My Typewriter Believes
Complete Twentieth Century Blues
Warrant Error

Edited
Floating Capital: New Poets from London (with Adrian Clarke)
News for the Ear: A Homage to Roy Fisher (with Peter Robinson)
The Salt Companion to Lee Harwood
The Door at Taldir: Selected Poems of Paul Evans

Criticism
Far Language: Poetics and Linguistically Innovative Poetry 1978–1997
The Poetry of Saying: British Poetry and Its Discontents 1950–2000
Iain Sinclair
When Bad Times Made for Good Poetry

Berlin Bursts

ROBERT SHEPPARD

Shearsman Books
Exeter

First published in the United Kingdom in 2011 by
Shearsman Books
58 Velwell Road
Exeter EX4 4LD

http://www.shearsman.com/

ISBN 978-1-84861-135-1

Contents

THE HOUSE OF OPPORTUNITY

after Michaël Borremans

Rows of red-shuttered windows
Open across the face of the House

Into dark orifices or into
Shaded living spaces

For his fingers or for the figures
Playing themselves

Without purpose he thinks
He places his hands before him

For this private lesson
Without compulsion harbouring music

A white-scarfed woman and perhaps three
Others walk from its shut green door

Away from marble steps as though
They've been expelled to scale

This thing up in its watery solidity
Transport it

To a landscape under veils of cloud
Torn from the pages of art

By a wooded hollow flecked with gulls
In any space it fills the House

Houses itself like a song
While the people who are dwarfed

Or dwarf it like him draw
Toward purpose

Pooled in their own shadows
Or drown waist-deep in discovery

EROTIC ELEGY

after Sigismunds Vidbergs' 'Revolution' (1925)

You thrash open the thick
Curtain interrupted we see

The troops bayonets
Fixed for entry they howl

For your sacks of gold
I moan for your reserves

Of desire both buried
I pillow against you breasts

Plumped in my shift
Brutal daylight

Shafts the length of my smooth
Legs from cool thigh

To bejewelled heel as I
Touch your arm I feel

You're ready to split and
Spill but we tremble as one

Providential storks on
The drapery shake

A pane crashes somewhere
I know they'll crack open

My curves like a shell
They're weak with war my

Enriched lips captive on
Your captured plush will

Offer full account in
The speech of the Phoenix

That now I see is what smoulders
Upon the auspicious drape

A PASSION FOR THE REAL

after Solomon Nikritin's 'The People's Court' (1934)

Both of his fists
locked

over the spread pages
of the stiff book,

sporting a smock
of black smoke

across the stage
upon which I will make

no show, he
is the People playing

its part. His guards
glance aslant

from the table's skirting
shadow. His clerk

is a fog of fingers
fixing his script with prompts.

But his deputy
twists round:

extemporal knocks
on the door

which yet may quicken all
of our exits.

Berlin Bursts

Looking Thru' a Hole in the Wall

                            don't
Destroy history spirited

Into the tainted air remains as
Its remains

Derelict monument to extra-human
Scale on sale as Pirate

Art gritting gritted
Teeth, mood

Recognitions across vacant
Division   balancing the hollow

Cusp of the wall a single
Book fans its open pages out

Of range of binoculars
Glass coffin temples &

Ghettos De Luxe—
Film escapades point

To posterity the shell of the
East & its visionary balconies

Out of Range

Sputnik on a stem
A boulevard of saluting

Tanks the unsecret head-
Quarters of the police ranked

Sweet jars
Of sweaty sex-swabs crazed

Dogs randy on the stink snap
At loins squeezed at gun

Point from worm holes a gift
Culture of the *nomenklatura*

The sheathed
Pleasures of ceremonial

Swords trumped up awards
Bookend Lenins &

Honnekers the dark stain
Of Directorate walls a narrow

Bed for the ultimate
Sacrifice squat telephones

Kept in the
Dark a bulky reel

To reel rolls out of an
Empty cocktail cabinet

Guarded gossip swivels
In ersatz

Modernity the
Reels spinning clacking

Spools a worthless archive
Of whispers

Sachsenhausen

1

Photographs of dogs guard the
House prices the dead

Make quiet neighbours he follows
The pilgrimage flapping in

White suit pursuit ponder the
Death March he catches

His breath his captive
Echoes repeated witness of a

Cover-cost testimony forever
Under the *Arbeit*

2

Watchtowers constrict the
Horizon granite slabs

Polyp'd with pebbles bodies
Tipped

From carts down basement chute no
Body speaks tiled room *preserved*

In shivering chill of doctors
Too scared to descend

To select tattoos on
Backs for science born

In guts outnumbered
By silence fresh

On the marble slab runnels
And sluices for human

Blood nobody looks in another's
Eyes colour

Coded receptacles for
Variegated garbage the

Clump of hair ghosting
A scalp

3

Wasp tormented rubbish bin a
Mausoleum of Coke cans that

A woman photographs a
Museum of extermination

Vitrines of stars nobody
Speaks to cover the ground

Crumbling splinters the Gestapo's
Green Casino abandoned

Strapline of hope *Mach
Frei* entering here the

Murmuring memorials over
The haunted shifting sub-soil

Dorotheenstädtische Friedhof

                    never grow

Patient huddled in
Holes or

Driving to the Ensemble
In *whose* car

Overlooking
The war-pocked graves

His modest prospect of
Hegel's block & of his

Own slab a stone for
Heartfield who swallowed *blech!*

The quiet families
Moving and pointing *there!*

They say to a scrubby
Flowerbed third stone no

Tombeau but plot of un-
Weeded earth for unnamed

Thinker permeated
With pessimism remembrance

Spurs Art
Fights my manuscripts Brecht

Wrote my suitcase lies in
Guiltless guilt

Riga Duet

Prison Camp Violin

A brittle fiddle someone
Turns this on a lathe

Of the spheres where
Replica becomes the real

Thing thin
Birch treated knocked up

Catches an unhuman
Voice in its hollow

Thumbs moulded to pegs
Skewered into splitting holes

Tune the stolen wires a
Mollusc curled at neck's end

Fingernails
Pluck the kinked tune free

Out of itself a
Collapsed bridge

Sabotaged by
Time mittens

Grapple
The soup-bone bow-grip

Horse hair human
Hair taut straight like a well

Brushed bride's
Bends the tamed twig

Tucked under your chin the violin
Splinters against your jaw

As you draw the grinty
Voice out from the mechanics

Of survival: extinct
Livonian love song

Mute Piano

This box could house
A stethoscope or

Paintbrushes its
Leather strap sags

A conspiring smile
Unclip the lid in

A double-thumbed
Ritual of rhyming

Clasps and prop
It open a jack-

In-a-box grin of black
And nicotine octaves

Three there potential
But one key escaped

Gives the game away
A peep-hole to the void

Imagined
Mechanics
          beneath

Coal-grained
Half-frozen fingers that

Soothe the smooth keys
And then in a furious

Double-fisted cluster
Rattle them with the

Padding stealth of
Rats upon boards

Stealing moist bread
From mute mouths

RATTLING THE BONES

for Adrian Clarke

The rest is history. Filling. The holes. The El Grechko Fresco
in Wenceslas Square

Hang gliding into the Palace of Wisdom pussyfooting around
the footmen transvestite torturers carnival butchers

: hands of Czech students grasping darkness of alcove fresh flowers
wreathed through twisted fingers

Take a machine gun to write. Britannia on square wheels
clunking iambics. The sculpted purity of a well-wrought fake
you could pass water through

Genuine. Aslant. Blood rags on the library steps. During the
stifled cough

> *What is recordable of paying attention I just don't buy*
> *That exchanged in a free market of speech it's*
> *Cheap talk at the national*
> > *rate the word crusade*

Each thonged delight receives its vote. They rub their own
wounds with sacramental dust. They fill a vacant chair with

a kiss-sculpted vapour of waste. Either way you're thrashed down in the bargain basement. Sings a cracked sphere within the cosmology of its own ringing endorsement

Flinty resistance of your floating. Voice thrown into becoming. 'Yours'

In which case what is the point. Are 'we'. Sleepless next. To the torture room in the mirror. Watch the reverse image moves backwards across the pain

Of neighbours one hundred and forty eight million of whom died when the narratives were merely grand. What can compete with this. When there's sugar on each table

The Peasant (*shoulders the dream but that dream isn't hers under Sentence of dearth*
                                        the phrase)'s Revolt

Committing these acts of writing

The cracked arteries of those metaphors we travel by   an abandoned filling station whose forecourt is spattered with blood

and as soon disappears a vapour I can neither hold nor contain
a reflection of a woollen sky in a rainbow puddle

at the city limits of Velopolis there are no limits) the horizon
disappears) you're examined by the evidence and left an 'open'
verdict

The history of the body as disembodied theoretic. The body
of history. With extra mouths for extraneous stories. Extra
months. Incorporated. U-topian calendars

or fresh orifices. Torn in the flanks of the dying animal.
Doubling as sexual mouths that sigh another man's trick. To
trick words out. As we re-articulate our limbs. Do we not
shred fat from our tongues. If I track everything back. To more
deaths than my own. The micro-gulag of gristle. Isolated by
gargantuan rivers of sweat

If man (ever) dwelt poetically

                              the blood song pumping
              'With the broken lyre between his hands,' sings
              Every poet since

                        sense-buds burst on the membrane. That
separates. *Unheimlich Volk.* That substitutes. A path across the
flesh hills. An exposure to the other. It is signification watch

the flowing. A substitution is separation. That is responsibility. Lashed to the eye let joy flood. Proximity. Which invulnerability. Pulses for a final drift. Of delight licking each other's tongues. After their longings. Journeys elsewhither home

By September 12th the Inside is on your face. Carnival excavations. Now. That utopianism is their way of lifting the shattered visage. Material breaches represent (how) the West that made representation present. A present which cannot be refused. Indelible delivery

Saying. The looseleaf epic is bound. To be netted. The realist's morning prayer we interrupt

This broadcast which is a broadcast of
Interruptions. To bring you
                              more complex nervous systems

that can never be reduced. To the plot. A fatal breath in the sentence of the condemned. To refuse. If not. To refute

in a mean time bodies as things you pull out of rubble

In its self for its self. The body itself. As itself. In itself on itself. Out of itself. Ecstatic reunion with its self *is* is the si-

ngularity as touch

of fur prickling
static

'to create
new connections
new linkages
or vital
transmitters in
the brain

(skeletal sonnet for adrian clarke

atomic
wordage
in
complex
counts

tangible
making
cumulatively
particularized

rigorous
finds

shifting
in
sites

November 2002–February 2003

A Voice Without

To say and not say at
the same time, or

at a different time to not
say and yet say—

eversaying, yes-
saying, gainsaying,

truthsaying, lying,
neversaying so that it

closes into what has been
said; to say that I

am not saying, to not
say that I am not

saying, or at a
different time to say that

has been said, but *this*
will never be said, quite

simply, quite inexplicably,
has never been nor gone,

has arrived without arriving
at what has been, has left

without leaving what is known,
disappears into the unknown

which is left behind, as
never before, said.

VOICES OVER

The brown brickwork
of the distant sanctuary

remains wall-eyed, but memory
slices its line

through the woods
from the trees, enters

the scratched
tunnel worming

where red lips
stick on the darkness,

a promise about to be
broken, or shadows

as the blind light
shears across

an escaping runway, the
fish-tail of a jet plunging

into fog, makes up
a face that prints

its human evasions on
the page I

live on
on time

through which I sink until
it freezes,

dancing angelic across hoisted
antennae in the valley, blots the

already frosty reception, knowing
the mystery of what's over

the hill keeps me,
the shock of spinning the dials

to find exactly what's
needed now: the word *dove*

printed above the picture
of a pouncing tiger.

THE POEM IN THE BOOK

Pines spear the sky but a pond's reflection up-ends them,
sucks them into itself. You'll never finish reading
the poem in the book with reality pulling itself
inside out before your eyes. You spread into darkness,
like unfurling capillaries, dissipated with love, several disasters
past the credit-crunch. It invests your vision with thoughty things:
the cool curves of her shoulder blades bunching before you
as a memory would, to obviate the mercantile distractions
of the city's edge-land centre. Is the beautiful woman still
beautiful when she blows her nose? Hoovers poke around shelves
and fittings that have not been sold to last customers
in hundreds of boarded-up branches. Hovering over books
patched with price-tags you're surrounded by people who
stand talking, not buying, participating in history,
dreaming of nothing that waking could provide.
You brush your way past their final scanning. New
euphemisms fill the skies with what isn't war, to carry
this fiction to you and keep stories on their toes.
When they're over, what's left? The sneeze of a lover
after sex, or a weave of cheap yellow paper flaking, dime store
superheroes in schoolboy code? Whichever account
leaves the poem it leaves the poem in the book,
in its way unwritten once more, beyond exchange,
in debt alone to pure winter light and blanket forgetfulness.

Roosting Thought

What makes us different is that we *talk* about our difference

We looked at the things, we listened to our minds, we sensed the beyond

The rightful protozoa slipped through our sticky fingers. The wilderness years

You've got to start with the wild rose growing wilder than ever, under cover of the unclipped hedge, a nesting nettle

A utopia all place and no people

There's a poem out there shooting the rapids, selected to win. A poem that hoovers up dead leaves and compresses them as desiccated veins of golden sunlight, moulds them into the mould as a fruiting star

Your Muse shimmies among dried pods on stalks, a clanking shimmer. Her dress is made of metal petals

Envine the brackets of experience and the writing exfoliates. Dull beasts munch methodically until all is naked world again, clear as the clearing where you park your Volkswagen for an icy skinny dip in the source of it all

Now it's time you named this world, this ring of shaking elms where the hill fairies sing or the Devil offers you porridge if you dance like a circus bear backwards

What happens over the hill is written off. A gospel on dry leaves to line your nest

The poet, leached out
of the cycle of meat for

one moment, looks back
at the wound, and names

his price. The
white page

forest of clearing throats

ANOTHER POEM

The scribe of the poem knows nothing
but he embodies every word you hold.
He's not an original. He's a solid
conduit, form rather than wave or
particle. He's left-handed, and his big
fist covers every word once it's formed.
The eyes he turns to us
                            in his mirror
                                    look away.
Careful not to smudge, he crouches low,
reversing the verse, furrowing his plough.
The poem tells of flowers and trees,
naming names you recognise from other
poems, but you can never make them out
in the wild. Did he say 'Wild'? No,
he didn't, as it happens. Neither did
the poem. You're making it up. You think
it should be you alone and the words
agreeing to differ. But you watch his fist
pounding the lines: *Alike the shuddering ball of
flame* or *Print regurgitated pulp.* The poem
has barely recovered from his scratches, yet
you're making to scribble links in its margins,
calming and charmless. Will you then tear
his calligraphy back, peel it off to leave
the wounded poem yours, a dripping pelt?
He fashions the final words. *Waves of feeling rush
towards this hooded moment.* His dream is to be power-
less as the endless poem.

                    Then he
inscribes, in mirror-script: *The scribe of this poem
knows it all*

YET ANOTHER POEM

Incalculable dispersions? The selves I
have a number. Of days now in an art
that is re-made as glaringly brilliant
banging. Art is unmade and laid to
restless drums, banging on about the glare.
Restless brilliance, all wrong, unmindful
in the acts of losing ruthless polarities
in place of space, sufficient ground. It
never lost on either or multiple sides, the
time before, for the setting was seen, a glimpse
of unscheduled action. Now lose the soft
fascination, the definite prosaic self. Losing
surface, the actors pause, surfing the poem and off
on stories, to a place to speak from, circum-
scribed, a stage cluttered with seating.
They have to be arranged to pull a gun
on you, forging a new space, new links.
On those link-sparky tracks, I
don't do that. I make art, unlimited
access, lightning surrogate gun making
language chains the unlikely. A
gun is pulled on the surrogate self, on
screens flat with dialogue, just once,
yards away. The abandoned Coke can
on the wall opposite attracts an art
in which the unsaying saying, once said,
sings. The 'you' that has effects, the
new audience, says again,
                              The props,
or the surrogate props, speak to themselves,
an uncanny overhearing

NOT ANOTHER POEM

after Krzysztof Ziarek

Often I am permitted to return to a field. And it is full of forces

Something is happening here, saying whatever, but saying all the same. But not. The same there's nothing to exchange. No need to

Forces don't build up in power. Or domination. A thoughtful, forceful relinquishing

Inside this field you are safe but not safe. All that is the world is not. The world. A bullet flies as the idea of a bullet (flies) but its trajectory is turned. To words like 'sleet' turning to 'snow'. To slow. It is a bullet that stands. In relation to every new thing

Everything here is transformed, every thing (out there) interrupted. A snow-bullet frozen mid-air becomes off-centre of a new constellation from where we see it transfigured our selves. What we think of it is the new thing

There's more of it. And more and more of it in a different way there's nothing. We can do with what we find here. It's not stock. This is where. I want to make some thing. Something elsed, but disavowed—disallowed, even—in this

A carafe, That Is a blue guitar. Beyonding art

I don't want to only make relations. I make. The gangly girl in black-framed glasses in my making. I make her trip back from her car to number 99 in her strappy party shoes to root out the Christmas present she has forgotten. Then I will make the thoughts she has as she returns

Outside of her there is domination. House numbers telephone wires. Humming with Power. Not poetry and its antinomies. Satellite navigation. Data shadow. Inside. They share the world is not escaped, but elsed

Empower me to be. So unpowered powerful. In my relinquishment by distance not elevation to keep the saying unsaid. To speak against is to speak. Let me do it I need to do it but let me speak something elsed. From somewhere else. Of something

I have *made* something. For you. Now you are someone else

POEM

The unmistaken girl and her
Shapely back take the

Poem, lift it off your tongue.
She passes and it pursues her

Brown shoulders shrugging
And the deep gorge of flesh

Stretching down her spine.
Desiring her sun-sheened

Back the poem waits; the lazy
Sky paints blank blue

Unhazed. At the kerb
Where she dances, her

Shadow shaves across a white
Sheet of street trash

Dazzling like blank
Paper. It stirs in starting

Breeze, rattles over cobbles,
Flips on its back, waits

To be tickled like a
Beast, or fed with her eyes.

The girl knows the part
She plays in this trick: a walk-on

In a poem about nothing
Much. She won't turn back.

She absorbs the poem like heat. It
Becomes her, she becomes

Its loss, its distance, turning cool
Into echo under the railway bridge,

A shadow, unscheduled,
Without a thing to throw it.

The accidental woman with the perfect
shoulders steals the poem
from my lips. She strolls past

and the poem follows her dark
rolling shoulder-blades and the long
hollow that enfleshes her flexing spine.

The poem wants her for its own.
The sun shines fierce, the sky
yawns deep blue unflecked with

white. In the gutter where her sharp
shadow sways, a discarded
square of hardboard, as blinding white

as the sheet of un-
written-upon paper before me now,
shivers in some freak gust,

slithers across the stones loose in
melting tarmac, clatters for her
to twist her body round. Yet she won't.

The young woman knows she is
but sun-glinted back glimpsed once in
a poem about something else

and refuses to turn. The poem she spirits
away round the corner, out of eyeshot,
tunnelled into shadow;

an echo of its unformer self.

TWIN POEM

A gloss between the lines
Identical to ours. This is the city
Of the stories you tell in narrowing
Testimony. Fragmentary pauses and shifts
Carried into the mind make credible things:
The light shimmering in the heat.
It is the pulsing gift which
Wakes in you a forgotten desire.
You will walk through the poem as though
Unfamiliar in that familiar life.

The executions become routine
But they are four hundred years too late
And in the wrong poem.
You watch me swallowed
Like an alien word that will not
Rise to love you wordlessly. Memory
Of this instant goes
Counterbeat to drum me out
To the regime of this place. People
Stride through the dark streets,
The squinted prose
The fifty men were hanged on
By the judicious wind.
Dreams stir and I
Lose their meanings in work so secret
A voice rises to lyrical soliloquy.

Make a world for you—
Only the promise of that world
Will be effaced
Before its recoil, silenced by the mind
Into its milky glare. The provisional

Government of each new word
Sets the bond men free.
I have given you eyes
Down there in creation. You're stopped
In the poem the sentence before
A roaring plea for possession and release,
An open verdict. When the words die, we die.

THE ONLY POEM (MENTZENDORFF HOUSE, RIGA)

The bearded woman with amber eyes
makes him tie elfin aprons to his shoes
which glide like galoshes over the polish
of the timbers while the bride's stilettos
tap-tap up the stairs without reproach or restraint

The women scraped away these walls
to reveal layered fauns and fountains
but when he plucks the harp that waits for him there
it lets off a slack dead sound. Escaping

their scrutiny he secrets himself in the mock
'Poet's Room'. The desk: a quill still rests across
parchment by a notebook embossed *Poesie*

He lifts the feathery pages loose from the flaking
leather spine to find that they are blank

As Yet Untitled Poem

for John James

I beg you to hear this boy. And hear him out.
His morning poem you're in, now,
is neatly creased as a crisp new shirt, stiff-
backed and clipped on its cardboard torso, posed.

It trips you over the cat from the film you've never
seen, as you search for your spectacles.
I use my enormous brain to seek the signals
they emit. We are both The Prisoner

on this island, Crusoes of overlapping surveillance.
Sleep is where we've come from, captive, a misty place
of drizzled desire and mordant fear. The fog has
lifted, real enough, for the expedition that must

set off for the explanation. Your house-
guest, a sort of vapour that
an opening door dispels, coughs his soft pardons.
Serious poetry is back in town:

the Unfinished *Alba* of the Unknown
Troubadour, whose *vida* is word for word. The
beloved of this lyric is the hero of that epic, where
sometimes I did seek, I beg you now to flee this boy.

THE HELLO POEM

for Alan Halsey

Hello poem, it's me again. I'm
the voice that lives upstairs. You

hear me reeling across my floor,
your ceiling, as I dance about my

affairs. And you about yours, not
miming my sound, un-

rhyming your eyes as they rise,
faltering, toward me, from the ground.

*

Hello poem, it's me again, the
other side of your world,

speaking long distance
straight

around your curve, racing
like a tycoon's jet

to overtake the dawn
and possess tomorrow.

*

Hello poem, it's me again. You
ran away with yourself to

stage your new self's forming. I am
the silence that inhabits your zero.

THE BIRD POEM

for Alice Lenkiewicz

Cormorant by the lakeside
Where the heron should be

As alert but hanging there
With wings half-unfurled

Like a man slipping a jacket
Down his back

Gulls with false eye feathered
Behind each real eye trot

To the freshwater and hop in
Geese side-step flat-footing

Their shit's verdure but that's
OK this isn't a nature poem

For not all the fowl are real
The Liver Birds cast into myth atop

The life assurance capitol preside
Over acts-of-god and credit-crunch

But the cormorant dived oily
Into saltwater once in imitation

Of its food's long flight. We
Did this and I found the words

Liverpool 2008

FROM HEPWORTH'S GARDEN OUT

for Rupert Loydell

In the dream (2008)

my father lives in the small town made famous by the painter
who once lived there. While he goes shopping for food, the
rain becomes torrential and floods the inside of the door,
dampening the drapes, and under it a pool spreads across
the varnished floorboards and collects between them. Later,
in company, the talk turns to art. One man speaks of the
painter, uses the word 'crèpelle', but I don't know what it
means, though I feel I ought. But when he collects nibbles
from the coffee table, I notice the bottoms of his trousers curl
round his shoes like elephant trunks, empty sleeves, sodden
from the rain. Open on the table is a large thick book. Peering
closer I see that it displays an alphabet designed by Eric Gill. I
think it odd that on the record player is Berio, whose music—
tinkles interrupted by crashing drums—ill-fits this ambience.
Indeed, I am dressed in clothes in the style of the painter. I
take off my sandy overcoat, with its fur collar, to reveal a jacket
and waistcoat and trousers, all in the same sand yellow with
a hint of mustard, and thin red stripes. The cut is distinctly
Edwardian, something of Algernon Moncrieff or Rupert Bear,
but I feel perfectly at ease. I know I ought to be able to wear
them in everyday life, outside of the prose I have now written.

In the garden (1981)

the woman plays bo-beep
between sculptures

like she does
in another poem

behold
the abandoned studio

a single light-bulb
hanging on a wire

like it might
in another's drawing

the untouched marble
aloof in fecundity

pregnant with itself
with unfinish

we pull at it our mass
pulling at its centre

but it won't budge
not even in this poem

where nearly anything
could happen

In the painting (1932)

the surfaces pile
plates

obscuring one another
drawing apart as one looks

the shadow of the
queen's profile

spills like hair
onto the stepped planes beneath

the colours of winter pasture
rubbed and smeared

grazed but glazed
frames half-drape frames

one shows horizontal
alternations (a beach rug)

another the sea uncertain uneven
blue cut by live-wire sun-crests

and a shallow field of sprouting
bathers

the queen gathers
her own place but her crown

shifts off into scribble
on a smoky headland

space grows impatient
to lock image

to reconfigure its dominion—
the relief of flats

TENTATIVES

for Roy Fisher at 80

Between buildings brushed
By bitter wind

Bodies chatter
Chilled equivocation

Sliced by splintered screen
Of sinking reflections

As some else
Thing resonates

A minor chord
Among flurries tinkling

Lost in
Tingles of thing

Hoist from the purest
Lyric a catch

To pull up the stepped lines
Silvered in living daylights

A neck ridged with bone barely
Turning on a pillow breathing fast

Obstinate anchorage
Slowly

Turning

Wind cuts sunlight
Leaf-glitter tells you it's there

Pushes so hard it could bend
Light if you chose to believe

      which you do it makes it
      cowl like a bush in a gust curling

Into its own grey withdrawal
Terrified of its black heart

Sun's low disk
Sinks

Throws long shadows lawns of
Dark stretching back from flaming

Brickwork the faces of buildings
Distant towers

Glint buckled fire for a
Second then gutter

Lost reclaimed
By the order of place some

Where at the periphery stretches
A god created by gospels

That thread between things
Like gossamer like culture

Six Poems Against Death

I am small against death and the mourning of history.
J.F. Hendry

Later Words on Human Unfinish

Grey screen
framed by window's edge,
a curtain's subtle incursion:

a veiled world
playing out singularities,
complexities. As it

darkens
you're drained by the glow
from the single lamp

Passers-by glance
to tease whatever configures from
the other side

Swift curtains
pull the edges of the world
close in

Later, in default,
synthesised voices:

utter apology in
human indifference

Later still,
prising

the eye
to the slit between

blank board walls,
regard within

the parched, the cracked
earth; desert:

the hard rhyme of
pairidaeza

Emailing the Dead

i.m. Bill Griffiths

Skeletal announcement
Summons up

    (the crack of bones
    the click of a mouse

Spectral email template
Pre-addressed to the dead one

Ready for our message
From imprescience

Thanatognomic
Ignorance

There's no end to it line-
Break its little one

The dead their own deity it's
Best to offer tactile thanks

Twitching under
Fingerprinting pulse

Little Shovel

for Iain Sinclair

To think through
The tune of the thing

To shiver with joy drive
Pattern against violence

Crueller than cruelty a
Quotation

Awaits new words
To fill it an allograph

Of utter utterance
Caught through the aperture

Of belonging longing
To think a moon

Pressing close to kiss the earth
Over the terraced hill

Dipping toward the turning river
To think outness contests

All the way the outline
Of a shadow that wasn't there

To think accident stumbles evil
Into the poem—

That 'little shovel' scooping his
Liver out to sizzle

—To think with particular and
Articular interruptions

Never to unthink skinned-in
Ecstasies in the poem that

Sees the world as well
As itself

Gravity Be My Friend

before and after Pipilotti Rist

, clouds shift

their weight on urban slush underbellies,
the white car bonnet

burns on a squint-edit, no secrets
this afternoon, the earth's map projected

onto heaven, in harsh sun car lamps
re-lit, blue chrome flash blinds me,

crouching grey-white wolf-clouds off,
passion rises in the body like barking

rock'n'roll, sways down the street,
a clarinet practises scales turning to a tune

of a thing from an open window, something
without a head goes head-over-heels,

grey pitted windscreen a shocked wash
of sudden rain, wipers scrape

temporary breach, configure
blotch-moments into solids,

event-sized shapes, both men in front,
loose ties around hot necks, the next clouds'

black rims fringed with greying and blueing,
she slows to light her cigarette, laconic,

steps to a kerb, leather bag over her
shoulder, it slaps her thigh, reminds her,

somewhere inside this body I'm happy, yes, she
walks across the ceiling with her red hair,

negotiating reefs of felt under window clouds,
climbs the ringed bark

into a sky of river,
cools her wrinkled feet

where fish turn to leaves and light, her hair-weed
in the half-tossed tide of the sky,

pulls away
like film that leaves me skinned, I step

from unwounded poise, as crystal light
bursts once more in the street, printing strips

that I peel from the surface of the world
with every newly-minted tread

Nieuwmarkt, Amsterdam

They stand in queues
as though death is rationed

We anatomise a pheasant
where such lessons are taught

on the dead, guts unrolled
to rule (in the painting);

where men are ringed by rope
and tossed into eternity—

we celebrate birth
with food, drink

They stand in line
where we split Tulp

from tulip. Only time
protects us from this—

again again again
we protest the human

with hunger, thirst

Sound

after Can Altay

The desert
at the centre
of the oasis

Dawn lifts light
from a darkened
page

as a white
sky tinted with hints
of blue

A burglar alarm
winks but later
a trembling loudspeaker

sunk in a mirror
gathers and
patterns the sand

2008

ON READING GERRIT KOUWENAAR

Grey light falls
over a grey page
as one sinks toward sleep
but barely avoids
the enveloping void
by sitting up straight,
breathing sharp air,
and reading, or re-reading,
a pleasured drift
that keeps one conscious
of language and its line
that one turns toward afresh
to let it carry itself
across one's bodily
attention, attenuated
string of sense, tense,
vibrant,
as one resonates oneself
and is moved and moves.

CRESCENT

The crescent as road, as building
following the road, as archetype

floating the skies, beyond cloud, rain,
rain silvering the paving like a snail,

and in daylight, sunlight even,
all colour blasted to silver streaks,

you walk the crescent and feel
its bias as torsion in the foot,

you stop by the steps that lead up
to Whitman's canary, abandoned,

yellow in the mind, as you push on,
clouds pull cover over the sun's weak eye,

in the crescent everything turns grey
until it shakes itself free

like a wet dog, and colours fluster,
flush back into the faces of things

that you face up to,
the pink cheeks of a timorous old woman

as you both wait for the traffic lights
to bloom

ON THE BUSES

after Jeffery Baker's video

The circuit is thrown open like a circus,
a confliction of tubes coiled into stress.

You're inhabited by its design, meaning
sucked out of the fluted bones of your actions.

Passengers with rubber gloves clean up their stories:
the stalker's red van *did* take the roundabout ahead

but coiled back to nose up behind everything you see,
a presentable set of windows cleansed by cloud

and a real cloth swallowed by an imaginary bucket.
Once the people clear out, everything is on display.

You hoist yourself over the seat, and it ceases to be a seat.
You're the after-image that is thrown off balance

between two black mirrors, a pneumatic bluster
twisting down the stairwell.

You thumb the red button on the yellow pole.
A sharp bell rings and the scene changes again.

The doors fold open, quite unlike wings.
You step off the buses at once, twice.

DAVE CAVE: HOLOGRAM POET

Dave Cave, Born Yesterday

Dave looks through his fake eye
And sees desire descending moist

Onto his ripe tongue its mute
Eulogies lapping aching

In the lexicon he swallowed like
Poor Peter the Metre before him

Dave has been programmed with
Everything a poet needs

Anodyne masochist with stainless steel
Ears a tungsten tongue

Moulded onto the lips he elopes
With adulterated language

Torn from fridge magnets
Marries it to his fuck-eye's

Possessions a handful
Of spongy breast a fistful

Of iambics chorusing *Welcome
To Our World* where anything

Like nothing can happen often
Dave eyes the local's universal

Challenged by pure cleavage
To name the punctuation mark

He most resembles in real life
His vocal eye unlids an Ode

To the eighteenth century Dash
A rakish barely syntactic glyph

—No grip on reality—holding nothing
Together like an unclasped bodice

Holding his own, out-programmed—
To rising squeals risible and bosomy

He dashes out—huskily chanting
Wordless husks—huffing

'Testing testing
Testing

Dave Cave, Sentient

Your shiny stockings speak
On Dave's dream planet

Light but no heat enfleshes
There's nothing to recover

You flirt with your own
Resentment shout abuse

Curl onto the floor now
Everything is his performance

A shiver down the spine of
Your dress shimmers like

Geese no laughter—squeals
Taxis honk like geese . . .

These patterns you make
Accidents in the big picture

The big story read as portent
Cows nibble the

Corner of the field as
Though lifting it free of Earth

This slice of unruly life
Works the world doesn't tune in

Until your body shudders
At dreams after a stirring

Thing that's wrong you feel as right
Dave's next stage of consciousness

Shuffles you into style
Steam rises from your soaked coat

Catching his its
Wanton clasp

On the bus you sit dripping

Dave Cave, CyberSocialite

Embedded in networking

He is lionised but fast
Outlines the theory of position

And disposition sensibly
Alert to both limits and possibilities

Not just of blue but the fire pictures
Of being wrapped in 'our' world

Those olive bodies just won't do
To be influenced by the future

Theories of subjectivation
The lunchtime meeting

Is spookily quiet with only the fox
A deep scar down its breastbone

Dave crouches over maps
Tilting at linguistic windmills

The floor is hardly covered
Focussing on the minutiae of the struggle

He says *I can speak for everyone*
I point out he can't after post

Dry-out immersions in selfhood a short
Week follows his long lost weekend

Dave, his Ode to Ruin

Animated reading YouTube

An algorhythm brushes
Dave's hair silver brings it to life

As we know it it's
Simple but no simpler

Than other technologies like
Thinking or putting our socks on

It's OK he won't
Feel a thing at least

Not the things which feeling
Inhabits unlike a real man thinking

Hologram poems he's a hologram
Making dead wheelbarrows for live men

To push up and down for special effect
His animated lips pucker

These things spittle foams
Along their rubbery rims

And orphic wisdom is dubbed a voice
Left over to claim like lost luggage

When the tide goes out
And the deck chairs are folded away

To prepare for Thracian flesh-meets
It chimes without charm

In 3D Dave is skin deep
All round and we've got eyes

In the back of his head and his
Poems arrive an unplanned progeny

A brood of Nietszchean moustaches
moist from shouting things most unkind

His prosthetic poetics sticks out
For trousered passion look him up

In The Fictionary of Notional
Bio-Forms and throw away the key

WOMEN SHE TELLS

Women she tells him
are gaming with this

name that soft palms
proffer

to stimulate their own
under the table

guest. A scene spare-
pricks her consciousness

too long to be perverse. One
undecided finger

doesn't make her
a man a woman

's unsure reward or
delirious punishment

to host the celestial bed-
springs! Breasting the hot

gushes she throws herself out
of herself. Gusted.

Displacing
himself, dis-

pleasured, her potent-
ial kick-start-kisses

become *his* gutsy part. He wants
to want a share involving her

involving her kind
of revolution.

He takes the parts
apart to long

where the longings now belong.
She spoons him into her mouth

with her long finger like like like un-
like the hints and gists

she wants him
to pick up, as he does. Along

the well-licked approaches to
her enshrined sphinx-smile,

her fondest
abuses tempt him

to bug her
automaton drag-kings.

Miracle

French is the language of angels
Light drowns bathes his death wings

Of excited voices agitate the air
Blind face swollen black tongue

Upon which a curse had once curled
As he climbed the ladder rushed

Absolution in dead words his uncle's
Whispered farewell in Welsh he played

His amateur part *I make myself*
A miracle a bishop held my feet

Truly Cragh died rises again he
Moves one toe then a hand then

Blood-blind eyes stare past prayer
Angels with soup bowls soap member by

Member he moves back into life
The bowels that soiled

His breeches on the scaffold
Twitch once more

                    once more
Where man's

Laws hold
Sway he bites

His bitten tongue the drop
Of Lady Mary's mercy turned

Off from the other side
Latin   French   *Saesneg*

Lord William glares
At his wife's rebel play-

Thing a bag of blood and shit he'd
Abandoned too soon

Cheated by her saintly
Entreaties he'd handed him

Over to her once
He was dead now

He is not but Lord William
Accepts Cragh's gift as soon

As he stops hating him the necklace
Of scabs binds them to eternity

BURNT JOURNALS

1924

for my father at 85

The city builds into sky, annexing uncharted
Everests. You hold the aerial photograph,
simplifying by geometry, distance, like Empire itself,
its Exhibition. Scots pipers grumble their way to Tut's Tomb.

A moment frozen in butter! The sculpted disaster
of Jack Hobbs bowled out! Hungry kids lick his creamy pads,
dreaming of tiptoeing across Margate sands for their annual.
The nose of the bike's side-car (hold on to your bonnet

Doris!) is an aeroplane of the motoring roads,
its spinning white-walls the prayer-wheels of modernity.
Hot-breathed from Colman's, Imperialists funnel

the rustling throng into atmosphere for a Saturday night
broadcast from His Master's Voice exhibit,
a dining room dominated by its cenotaph of sound.

1929

for my mother at 80

Doris takes the wheel of her big red motor.
Thin cherry lips launch her into sound though
her bare arms remain untinted as they signal.
A tram clacks before her, a puppet under wires.

Her city of the future stacks itself like crates:
a narrow sky full of flying ships and tri-planes.
The Imperial Airways Argosy stretches its wings;
the propeller sniffs the air as she boards for Paris.

Over England, she spies a train puffing under
a giant excavator, each truck loaded with gravel,
the slow turning of earth into a pit of electric sparks.
They'll illuminate the nation in the dark days to come.

Doris says the Flapper Vote will win it for Labour.
The Floral Clock once tolled a giddy sprig of heather.

1939

for Lee Harwood at 70

The sergeant under the umbrella splashes Bovril
as he carries a cup to the private on duty.
It's all part of the service of the services,
it seems, in this dream that you're marched into.

The Cenotaph crouches under billowing silks
as a new red bus putters up Whitehall.
The colony of Belisha beacons flashes in harmony
lukewarm but welcome like a pie.

Everybody's aunt assembles by the ambulances,
masks tested for when the city turns to mustard.
Their perforated snouts chorus submarine melodies,
rubbery inhalant hallelujahs! The last pleasure

boat is moored, the boathouse padlocked. Time
is serving time, commandeered for the duration.

1944

for Allen Fisher at 65

Eros nests in his war tent. A
sailor peeps from behind,
watches the American airman
striding along with Rose

as if they owned the circus,
ignoring the striped bollards,
rockets at a crossing.
Commandos clamber up

neat square rigging like
counters on a board game
Rose plays in black-out
after the alert. Later, she

pulls new nylons up towards
suspender-belt and forbidden frills
like a rumour of tangerines off
the ration. In silk slip, straps free,

she hums our only bunch
of coconuts. This must be Paradise
the way she feeds us *Khaki
Figures at the Base*

of the Bombed-Out Grammar School
kicking through brick-dust
and desks, dwarfed by a ghost
wall, making up the future:

a lesson in kitchen Technology,
crystal shining on glass shelves,
a tendrillar stool so Rose may perch
for those midnight snacks to come.

1949

for Gavin Selerie and Alan Halsey at 60

You walk away from the Dakota, its silver fuselage
creaking as it cools. You wave your summer hat
at futurity. A grainy artifice sells the peace,
white-feathered fall into history's nigrescent ink.

Heads of the crowd glow pin-pricked under *Schweppes* flashes
on a newsreel besmirched by mist. You sip real wine
under a tilted made-up parasol, an untitled poem
by Wallace Stevens, full of his tropical clickety-click.

You recite crisp leaves from the borders of the Floral Clock.
The Dummy Cowgirl Orchestra fumbles mandolins
with bloated plaster fingers, stares through golf-ball eyes.

Not quite as advertised, they flicker within without
voice. All these lovelies are lost in black.
Your pure ears ring with perfect pitch.

1969

for Peter Manson at 40

The bridge's girders droop between the towers
as families picnic beside the service station.
Boxed off by iron railings, the tutelary deity reclines.
His soul flows into the river's tributary, a paddling pool

abandoned after the national celebration. His
castle has been patched up, a big fist on an old map,
a rusty rock on the Atlantic. His radio telescope
swivels on its bottom. Astrolabe or thumbscrew,

his ritual knick-knacks rattle. His face thirsts
for an imaginary drought, spies out from his
monstrous ermine, its verdant contaminants.

The bridge rules its own horizon across the city
as tugs chug beneath. A tangle of wires scuttles
up the dockside, running on repeat forever.

SONG

for Patricia

Que tal se van d'amor gaban
Nos avem la pes'el coutel

Everything you offer creaks
at my fingers, grips the distance I'm

too hard. The body must be tended
tenderly, a quiet coming

covering your mouth. You
plump me up. You flirt

let the bob and the zip plunge safely
on my face. I lift my

self to my knees to be wrapped
over, fringing, liminal mound.

The veins in your neck tighten.
Your teeth taste your self.

We wriggle our tongues in each other's
spilling-over rather than reaching out:

a gentle invasion, the hollow still,
nosing back the sheets to find ourselves

through the mesh. Brushing over
I narrate myself, contract around

your heels making me tip on my toes
ready for spaces within, a face to

fall into, a body wrap. I cannot
see the smile on your face. I

could cry out at this moment large
tight buds for you. A little shudder.

Now you sink, I look at a blind eye.
It looks back, tight with song.

Acknowledgements and Notes

Some of these poems appeared, or are due to appear, in the following magazines and journals: *Agenda, Eyewear, Litter, Neon Highway, New Writing, Onedit, Pages, Poetry Salzburg Review, Poetry Wales, Shadowtrain, Skald, Softblow, Stand, Staple Diet* and *Tears in the Fence.*

Poems have appeared in the following anthologies: *The Other Room Anthology 2009; Troubles Swapped for Something Fresh.* ed. Rupert Loydell. Cambridge: Salt Publishing, 2009; in *Salamanders and Mandrakes: Alan Halsey and Gavin Selerie at Sixty,* IP Press, 2009; in *From Hepworth's Garden Out.* ed. Rupert Loydell. Exeter: Shearsman Books, 2010; and in *An Unofficial Roy Fisher.* ed. Peter Robinson. Exeter: Shearsman Books, 2010.

'Berlin Bursts' first appeared in *Looking Thru' a Hole in the Wall.* Liverpool: Ship of Fools, 2010, with images by Patricia Farrell.

'Not Another Poem' first appeared in the piece 'A Carafe, a Blue Guitar, Beyonding Art: Krzysztof Ziarek and the Avant-Garde' in *Avant-post: the avant-garde under 'post–' conditions.* ed. Louis Armand. Prague: Litteraria Pragensia, 2006, and is a response to Ziarek's book *The Force of Art.*

'A Voice Without' forms part of *The Anti-Orpheus: A Notebook* (Shearsman Books, 2004, available as an e-book at www.shearsman. com/ebooks/ebooks_home.html)

'The Poem in the Book' and 'The Bird Poem' were written for the *Neon Highway* credit-crunch reading at the Tate Gallery, Liverpool, January 2009.

'The House of Opportunity' was written as a response to Michaël Borremans' work in the exhibition 'The End of the Line' (The Bluecoat, Liverpool, 2009).

'On the Buses' was written for, and appeared in, the collaborative exhibition of words and objects made in response to works of art *In their own words* held at Bank Street Arts, Sheffield, 6 November–5 December 2009, in this case in relation to a video of Jeffery Baker's action/intervention of the same title. It was published in the catalogue *In their own words.* ed. Jon Clark. Sheffield: unlimited editions ltd (in conjunction with Bank Street Arts), 2009.

Thanks to the editors, publishers, curators and poetry activists who invited me, or incited me, to make these texts public.

Sigismunds Vidbergs' drawing 'Revolūcija' (1925) comes from the series 'Erotika' and is published in the collection *Erotiskās Elēģijas/ Erotic Elegies*. Riga: Valters un Rapa, 2002.

'Rattling the Bones/ for Adrian Clarke' is a response to Adrian's poetics piece 'Introduction in the form of an Open Letter to Robert Sheppard on Exile, Nomads & the Demon', in his *Skeleton Sonnets*. London: Writers Forum, 2002, which is itself partly a riposte to my 'The End of the Twentieth Century: A Poem for Readers and Writers' in *Twentieth Century Blues*. 'With the broken lyre between his hands' comes from David Gascoyne's 'Hölderlin's Madness'.

'Twin Poem' is twinned with 'Twin Cities', in *Returns*. Southsea: Textures, 1985. It is an 'unwriting'—'Unwriting 1' of that strand in fact—of the poem's drafts, composed on 14–15 August 1985 and revised on 14 August 2006. It nearly got away.

The painting in 'From Hepworth's Garden Out' is Ben Nicholson's '1932 (crowned head—the queen)'.

Six Poems Against Death was originally conceived as an extension of, commentary upon, the final six sonnets of *Warrant Error*, 'Out of Nowhere', and there is enough of that intention still remaining for this to be acknowledged. 'Little Shovel': the title refers to an event in the life of Tony Lambrianou, related in his *Inside the Firm*. London and Basingstoke: Pan Books, 1991. Pipilotti Rist's 2007 installation 'Gravity Be My Friend' (FACT, Liverpool, 2008) entered the writing of the poem of that title, but is not a description of that work; likewise, a viewing of Can Altay's 2008 sculpture 'Deposit (Spring Deficit: After Dubai, After Hammons, and after the politics of white noise)' (The Bluecoat, Liverpool, 2008) lies behind the sixth poem. In 'Nieuwmarkt, Amsterdam' the painting is Rembrandt's 'The Anatomy Lesson of Dr Tulp'. 'Pairidaeza' is the Persian word for a walled garden, the root of the word paradise.

'Miracle' owes to Robert Bartlett's *The Hanged Man: A Story of Miracle, Memory and Colonialism in the Middle Ages*. Princeton and Oxford: Princeton University Press, 2004.

The quotation in 'Song' is from Guillaume IX d'Aquitaine, and is freely translated as 'Others may gab about love / But we've got the fork and the meat.'

* 9 7 8 1 8 4 8 6 1 1 3 5 1 *